westermann

Bumblebee

Workbook 3
Förderausgabe

Herausgegeben von
Gisela Ehlers

Erarbeitet von
Michaela Schönau
sowie Gisela Ehlers, Anna Van Montagu,
Matthias Muth, Hannelore Tait

Auf der Grundlage der Ausgabe
Bumblebee 3 (2021)
von Gisela Ehlers, Anna Van Montagu,
Matthias Muth, Michaela Schönau, Hannelore Tait

Illustriert von
Juliane Assies, Oda Ruthe, Friederike Schumann
sowie Matthias Berghahn, Andrea Dölling,
Jutta Garbert, Angela Glökler, Heike Heimrich,
Gabie Hilgert, Elisabeth Holzhausen, Karoline Kehr,
Ulf Marckwort, Isabelle Metzen

Contents

TB	Textbook
WB	Workbook
CD	Teacher's Audio-CD
FC/WC	Flashcards/Wordcards
SC	Storycards
L	Lehrkraft
SuS	Schülerinnen und Schüler
Fö	Förder-Kopiervorlage
KV	Kopiervorlage

Rote Wörter stehen fest: Merke sie dir.
Schwarze Wörter kannst du austauschen.
So entsteht ein neuer Satz.

I'm 8.

I'm 9.

1 Aufgabe aus dem Anforderungsbereich I: Imitation, Reproduktion und Wiedererkennen

1 Aufgabe aus dem Anforderungsbereich II: Reproduktion, erste Konstruktionsversuche und Erkennen von Zusammenhängen

1 Aufgabe aus dem Anforderungsbereich III: Zunehmend eigenständige Konstruktion

- listen
- point
- talk/tell/speak/sing/practise/ask
- read/look up/look at/find
- write/fill in/label/number/circle/tick
- draw/colour/create/mark/complete
- match
- Work/Compare with a partner.
- Do a role play./Act it out.
- Play the game.
- language tip

Welcome

1 Höre die CD und zeige auf die Fotos.
Streiche die Fotos zu den deutschen Wörtern durch.

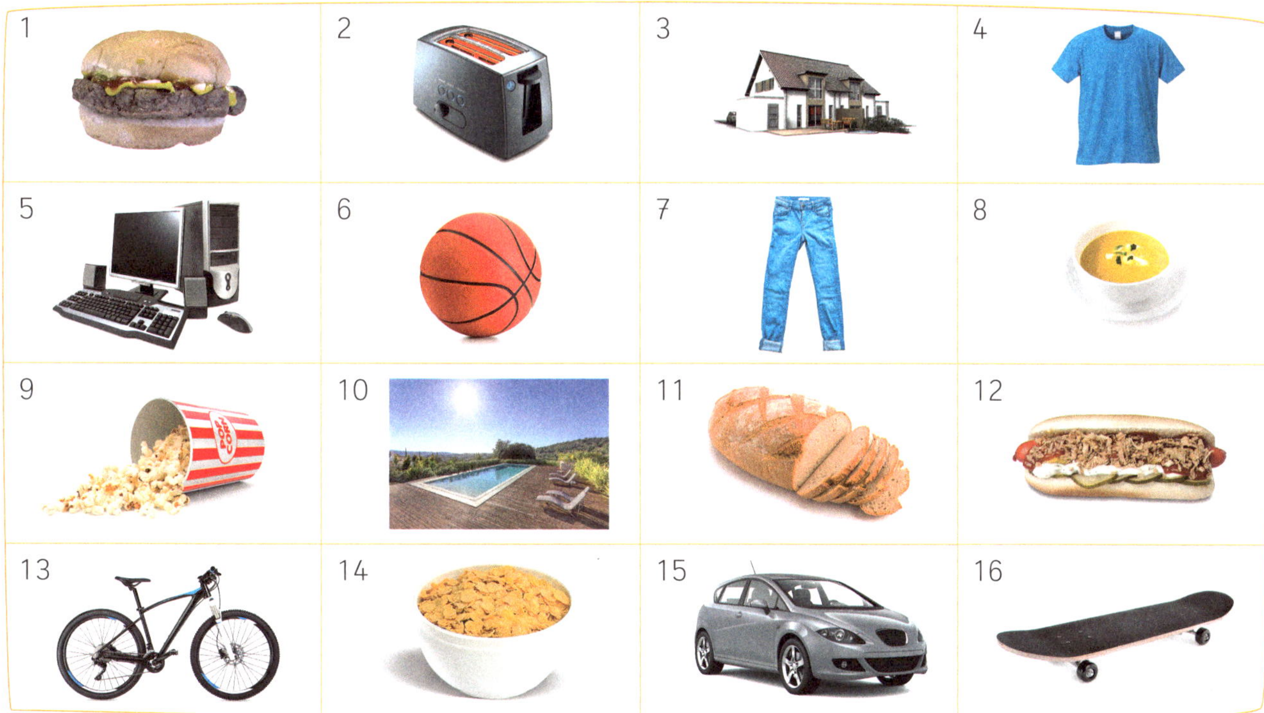

2 Lies und schreibe die richtige Nummer neben das Bild.
Vergleiche mit einem Partnerkind.

	jeans		hamburger		computer
	cornflakes	13	mountain bike		T-shirt
	basketball		popcorn	2	toaster
	pool		skateboard	12	hot dog

Nomen werden im Englischen klein geschrieben.

3 Umkreise die englischen Wörter.

shorts
ketchup
Schule
Hummel
song
laptop

Colours and numbers

1 Höre dir das Lied an. Zeige auf die Kreise.

2 Male die restlichen Kreise an. Singe das Lied.

( ) and ( ) , ( ) and ( ) , ( ) and ( ) .

( ) and ( ) , ( ) and ( ) , ( ) and ( ) .

And ( ) and ( ) and ( ) and ( ) ,

( ) and ( ) , ( ) and ( ) , ( ) and ( ) .

3 Höre die CD an. Male die Zahlen aus.

So schreibt man die englischen Ziffern 1 und 7.

0 1 2 3

4 5 6 7 8

9 10 11 12

CD 4-6
KV 6
Fö 2-3

LET'S PRACTISE!

About me

1 Ergänze die Fragen.

2 Lies den Dialog.

3 Übe den Dialog mit einem Partnerkind.

My name's = My name is

At school

1 Beschrifte die Schulsachen.

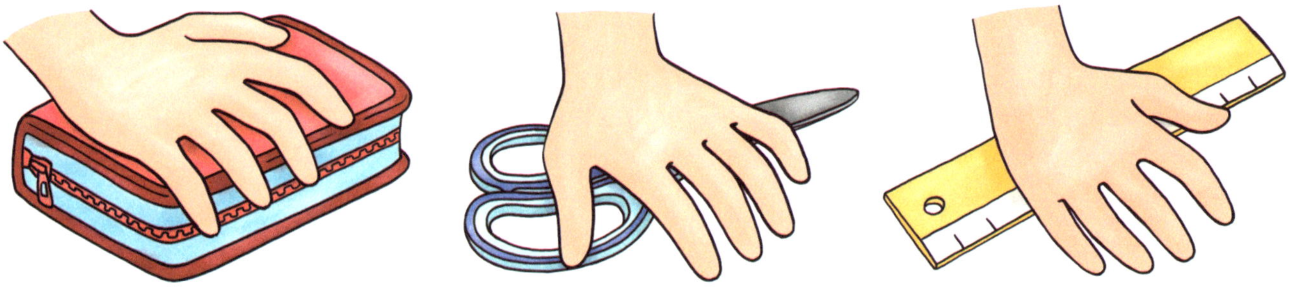

It is a pencil case. These are scissors. It is a r_ _ _ _ _.

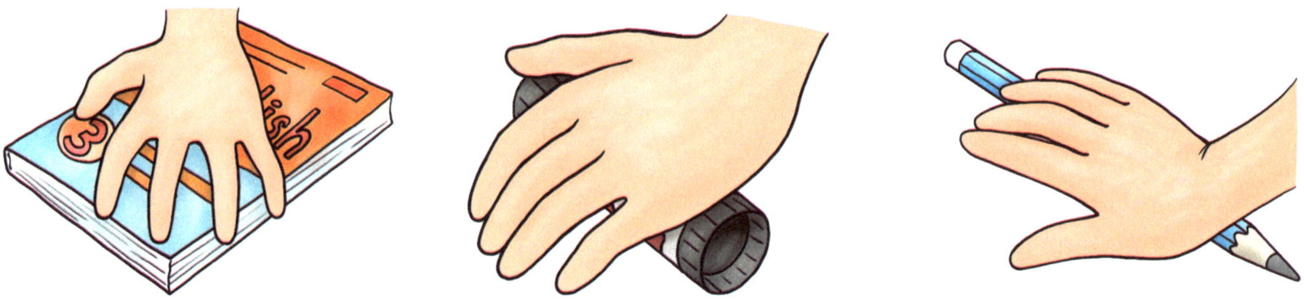

It is a b_ _ _ _. It is a g_ _ _ _ s_ _ _ _ _. It is a p_ _ _ _ _ _.

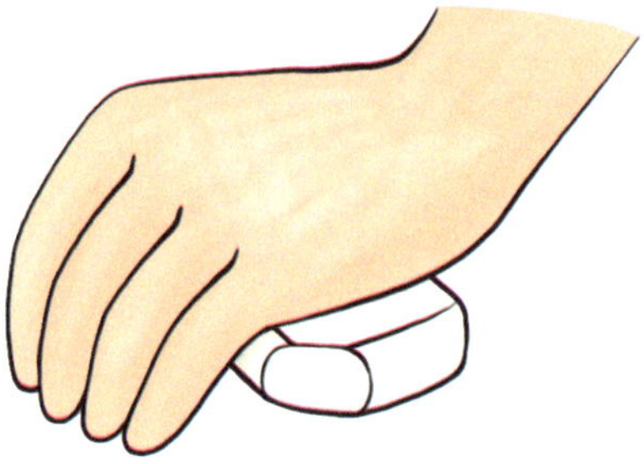

It is a r_ _ _ _ _ _.

~~pencil case~~ ~~scissors~~ ruler book glue stick pencil rubber

2 Spielt das Ratespiel.

Fö 4

LET'S PRACTISE!

Colourful school things

1 Höre die CD an und male die Schulsachen richtig an.

2 Überprüfe mit einem Partnerkind.

3 Lies und verbinde.

4 Mache ein Farbdiktat mit einem Partnerkind.

1 pen – 2 pen**s**

3 pens
5 pencils
4 rulers
2 rubbers
6 glue sticks

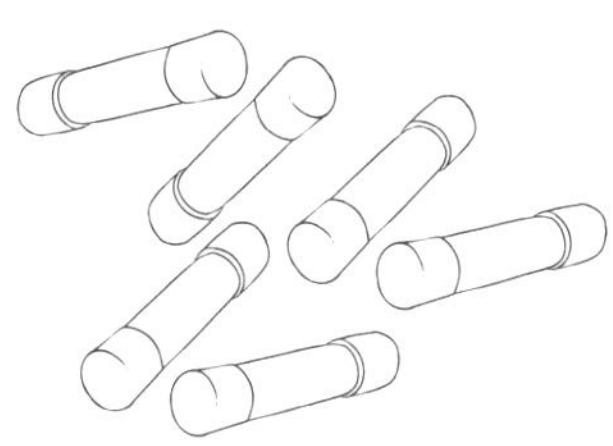

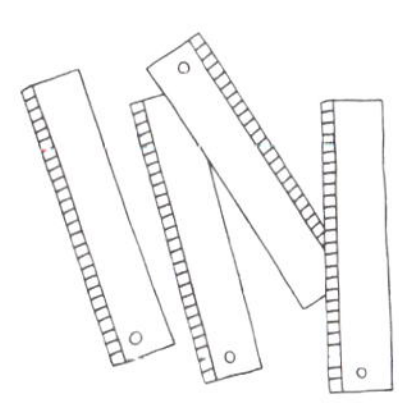

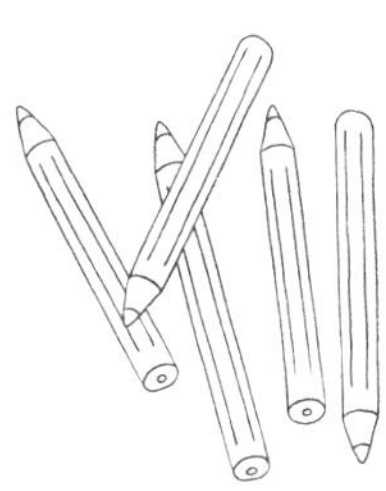

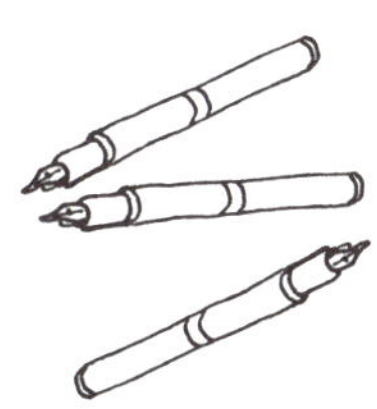

Shopping lists

1 Lies und nummeriere die Einkaufskörbe.

1
2 glue sticks
a green sharpener
a yellow folder
a red rubber

2
a blue pencil
a red pencil case
2 folders
a green rubber

2 Schreibe einen Einkaufszettel für den Korb, der übrig bleibt.

pencil | rubber | glue stick | pencil case

Honey page – At school

Schau nach auf den Seiten 5-8 im TB!

1 Das sind meine wichtigsten Wörter zum Thema Schule.
Schreibe die Wörter in den Rahmen, die du dir merken möchtest.

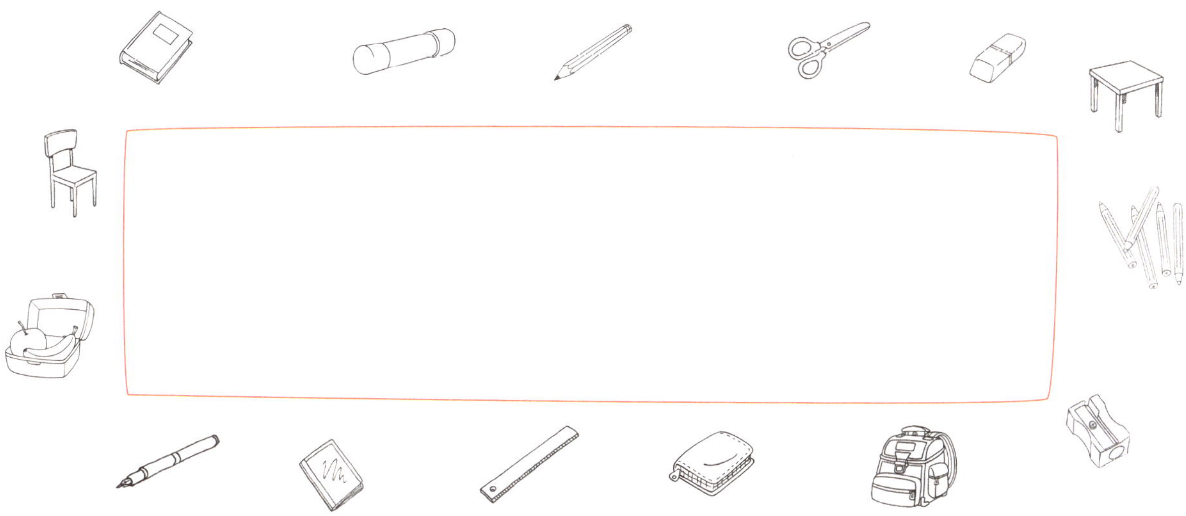

2 Ich kann um einen Schulgegenstand bitten.

3 Ich kann über mich berichten.

What's your name?	I'm fine/ ...
How old are you?	My name is ...
How are you?	I'm ... years old.

Lisa's new home

1 Finde die14 Wörter und kreise sie ein.

O	B	Q	**T**	O	I	L	E	T	C	B	**G**	W	W	A
I	K	V	Y	E	I	M	**W**	M	Q	L	R	A	E	L
S	**G**	E	R	P	P	B	A	F	Y	V	A	R	W	J
V	R	X	**L**	A	M	P	R	O	S	M	N	L	L	K
G	A	R	V	A	E	X	D	B	K	K	D	K	X	T
P	N	H	R	R	B	P	R	A	B	K	F	P	E	A
R	D	Z	**S**	O	F	A	O	L	I	E	A	H	K	O
B	M	L	W	X	I	G	B	**S**	I	S	T	E	R	**B**
P	O	B	N	N	M	S	E	I	W	Z	H	B	K	R
B	T	B	W	K	**B**	O	O	K	**S**	H	E	L	F	O
H	H	H	**F**	R	I	D	G	E	H	U	R	I	Y	T
V	E	**M**	O	T	H	E	R	T	O	G	V	E	E	H
A	R	K	U	C	X	W	E	T	W	B	E	P	**B**	E
I	O	S	T	G	**F**	A	T	H	E	R	L	W	E	R
G	R	H	N	I	W	Y	B	U	R	I	W	M	D	O

→	↓
~~toilet~~	~~grandmother~~
lamp	wardrobe
sofa	shower
sister	grandfather
bookshelf	bed
fridge	brother
mother	
father	

2 Schreibe die richtigen Wörter zu den Bildern.

family

f ____________

m ____________

b ____________

s ____________

g ____________

g ____________

house

s ____________

l ____________

b ____________

w ____________

s ____________

toilet ____________

f ____________

b ____________

LET'S PRACTISE!

Find the furniture

1 Verstecke alle Möbel und spiele das Spiel mit einem Partnerkind.

	 toilet	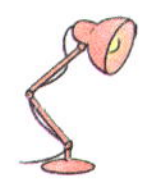 lamp	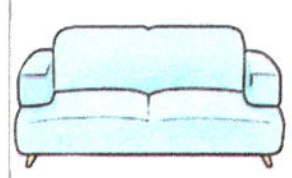 sofa	 bookshelf	 fridge	 wardrobe	 bed
kitchen							
hall	X						
bedroom							
living room							
bathroom							

2 Schaue dir deine Lösungen aus Aufgabe 1 an und vervollständige die Sätze.

There is a ____toilet____ in the ____hall____.

There is a ____________ in the ____________.

There is a ____________ in the ____________.

There is a ____________ in the ____________.

Lisa's family

1 Höre die CD an und zeige auf die richtigen Bilder.

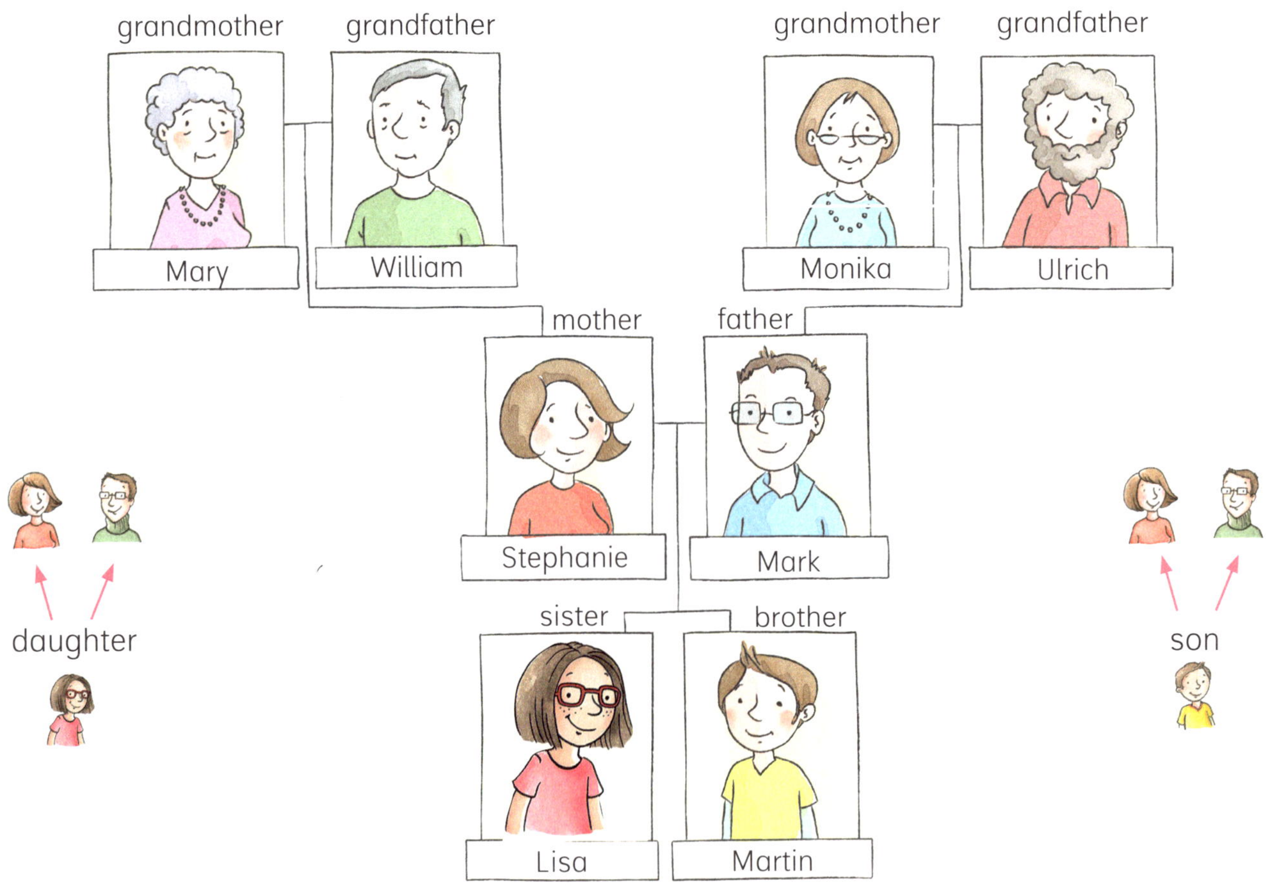

2 Vervollständige die Sätze.

Monika is Lisa's grandmother.

Ulrich is Lisa's g

Mark is Martin's f

Stephanie is Lisa's m

Martin is Lisa's b

Lisa is Martin's s

CD 20

Small families – big families

1 Lies die Texte und verbinde mit dem richtigen Bild. Die Schlüsselwörter helfen dir. Schreibe den Familiennamen ab.

Park

The Wilson family is a big family: father, mother, two sons and two daughters.
They have got a dog.

Wilson

The ______________ family is a small family: mother and her son.
They have got a hamster.

Green

The ______________ family is a big family: grandfather, grandmother, father, mother and a baby daughter.
They have got a cat.

Khan

The ______________ family is a big family: grandfather, father, mother and a son.
They have got a dog.

Where is ...?

1 Lies die Wörter und beschrifte das Bild.

computer chair ~~bed~~ table wardrobe lamp teddy bear football

2 Beantworte die Fragen.

~~in~~ next to in front of on behind on

Where is the pullover?

The pullover is in the wardrobe.

Where is the teddy bear?

The teddy bear is n ______ the wardrobe.

Where is the lamp?

The lamp is b ______ the bed.

Where is the computer?

The computer is o ______ the table.

Where is the chair?

The chair is i ______ the wardrobe.

Where is the football?

The football is o ______ the bed.

Fö 10-11

Honey page – Lisa's new home

1 Das sind meine wichtigsten Wörter zum Thema Räume und Möbel. Beschrifte alle Gegenstände, an die du dich erinnern kannst.

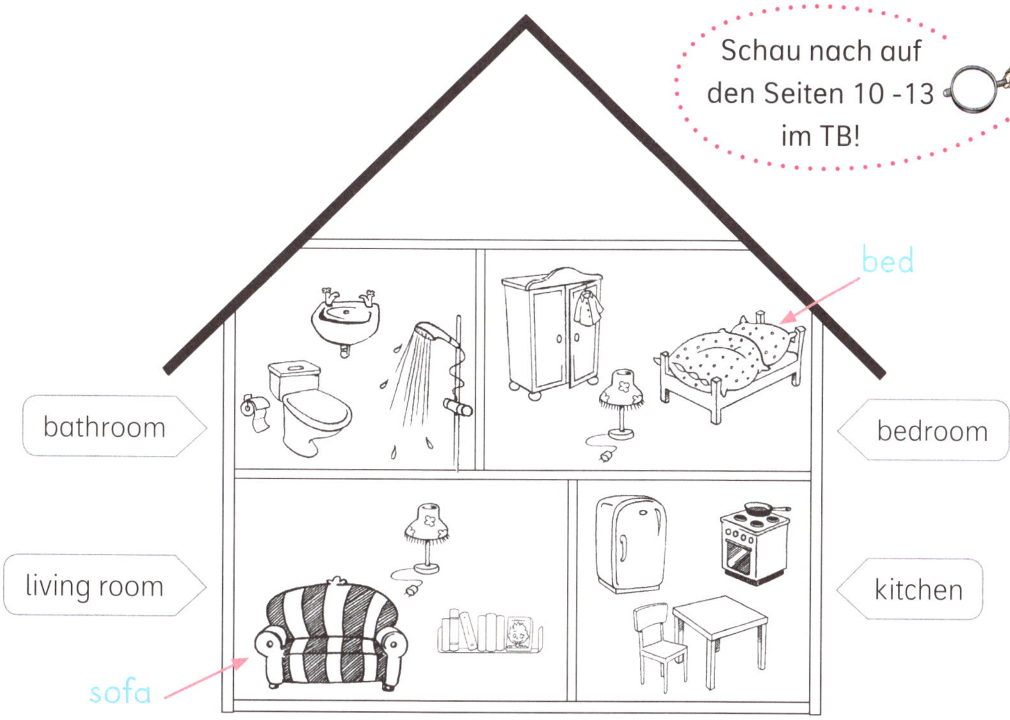

2 Ich kann sagen, in welchem Zimmer welche Möbel sind.

The sofa is in the living room.

3 Ich kann über meine Familie berichten.

Free time

skateboarding, swimming, drawing, reading, playing hockey, dancing, meeting friends, biking, playing cards, horse riding, collecting stickers

1 Löse das Kreuzworträtsel.

2 Ergänze die fehlenden Buchstaben.

1	2	3	4	5	6	7		8	9	10	11	12	13	14	15
		a			n		☆					b			

3 Vervollständige den Satz mit dem Lösungswort von Aufgabe 2.

My favourite hobby is ______________________________ .

KV 34
Fö 12

Favourite hobbies

1 Was sind ihre Lieblingshobbys? Höre die CD an und umkreise die richtigen Bilder.

Ben

1. biking

2. reading

Ben's sister Louise

1. playing computer games

2. playing football

Ben's father – Mr Marley

1. meeting friends

2. playing an instrument

Ben's mother – Mrs Marley

1. watching films

2. playing tennis

2 Schreibe die Hobbys von Bens Familie auf.

Ben's hobby is biking.

His sister's hobby is p_______________ f_______________

Ben's father's hobby is p_______________

His mother's hobby is w_______________

LET'S PRACTISE! When can we meet?

1 Höre den Dialog von der CD an und lies mit.

1. Stelle die Frage und drehe die Flasche.

2. Beantworte die Frage. Stelle die nächste Frage und drehe die Flasche.

3. Nimm dir eine Bildkarte und beantworte die Frage.

2 Spielt das Spiel in einer Kleingruppe. Benutzt diese Wörter.

meet some friends 

play football 

play tennis 

go biking 

go swimming 

play cards 

dance 

play hockey 

go skateboarding 

listen to music 

CD 41
KV 38
Fö 16

Days of the week

1 Schreibe die Wochentage in der richtigen Reihenfolge. Ergänze die Kurzformen.

Saturday	Monday	MON	TUE
~~Monday~~	T		FRI
~~Thursday~~	W		~~MON~~
Sunday	Thursday	THU	~~THU~~
Wednesday	F		SAT
Friday	S		SUN
Tuesday	S		WED

2 Lies und verbinde.

Hello, I'm Lucy.
My favourite hobby is skateboarding.
On Wednesday I go skateboarding with my friends.

My name is Shan.
My hobbies are playing table tennis and swimming.
Every Sunday we play table tennis in the garden.

My name is Meena.
My hobbies are biking and horse riding.

My busy week

1 Lies die Wörter und verbinde sie mit den passenden Bildern.

play football

go biking

play computer games

go swimming

go horse riding

meet friends

play table tennis

play basketball

play hockey

go shopping

2 Schreibe über deine Woche.

On Monday I ______________________________

On Tuesday I ______________________________

On Wednesday I ______________________________

On Thursday I ______________________________

On Friday I ______________________________

On Saturday I ______________________________

On Sunday I ______________________________

3 Sprich mit einem Partnerkind über deine Woche.

Honey page – Free time

1 Das sind meine wichtigsten Wörter zum Thema Hobbys. Schreibe die Wörter in den Rahmen, die du dir merken möchtest.

Schau nach auf den Seiten 19 und 23 im TB!

swimming,

2 Ich kann meine Lieblingshobbys aufzählen.

My favourite hobbies are ____________________

____

3 Ich kann mich mit jemandem verabreden.

1 Can we meet on ____________ ?

2 Sorry, on ____________ I ____________ .

3 What about ____________ ?

4 Okay, let's ____________ on ____________ .

Pets

1 Höre die CD an und kreuze das richtige Wort an.

◯ goldfish ◯ cat 	◯ mice ◯ hamsters 	◯ mouse ◯ cat 
◯ rabbit ◯ cat 	◯ mice ◯ guinea pigs 	◯ dog ◯ guinea pig 
◯ cat ◯ dog ◯ hamster 	◯ dog ◯ guinea pig ◯ rabbit 	◯ budgie ◯ mouse ◯ rabbit 

2 Finde die Haustiere und kreise sie ein.

3 Schreibe die Haustiere auf.

G	A	**B**	U	D	G	I	E	R	K	**D**
O	B	G	M	Q	U	**H**	A	E	L	O
L	**G**	U	I	N	E	A	☆	**P**	I	G
D	C	H	N	R	K	M	B	F	M	O
F	D	I	**M**	O	U	S	E	G	**C**	P
I	**R**	A	B	B	I	T	H	C	A	R
S	E	H	O	S	V	E	D	I	T	S
H	F	**M**	I	C	E	**R**	A	T	H	T

 → guinea pig

 → r

 ↓ c

 → r

 ↓ h

 ↓ d

 → b

 ↓ goldfish

 → m

 → m

LET'S PRACTISE!

What's your favourite pet?

1 Befrage die anderen Kinder.

What's your favourite pet?

My favourite pet is a cat.

	 dog	 cat	 rabbit	 guinea pig	 hamster	 mouse	 budgie	 goldfish	 rat		
Mia		X									

2 Sprecht in der Klasse über eure Lieblingshaustiere.
Findet die beliebtesten Haustiere.

The most popular pet is the ______________________

Pets in class

1 Höre die CD an und nummeriere die Bilder.

2 Lies und trage die fehlenden Wörter in die Lücken ein.

~~grey~~	~~four legs~~	~~long tail~~	mice	cat food

The cat is grey. It has got four legs and a long tail.

It sleeps in a basket. It likes ________ and ________.

~~yellow~~	legs	short tail	cage	carrots

The hamster is yellow. It has got four ________ and a ________. It lives in a ________. It likes ________.

dog	brown	~~white~~	four	~~long~~	basket	bones

The ________ is ________ and white.

It has got ________ legs and a long tail. It sleeps in a ________.

It likes ________ and dog food.

orange	legs	fish bowl	fish food

The goldfish is ________. It has got no ________. It lives in a ________. It likes ________.

CD 47
KV 43
Fö 19, 21

The rabbit and the goldfish

1 Lies die Sätze.

2 Umkreise die Sätze, die zum Kaninchen gehören rot und die Sätze, die zum Goldfisch gehören grün.

My pet has got **four legs**.

My pet eats **fish flakes**. 

My pet lives in **a big cage**.

My pet has got **two long ears**. 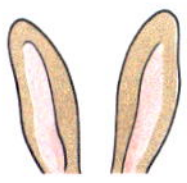

My pet lives in **a fish bowl**. 

My pet is **orange**.

My pet eats **grains**. 

My pet can **run**.

My pet can **swim**.

My pet has got **no legs**.

3 Schreibe drei Sätze zum Goldfisch oder zum Kaninchen ab.

All about my favourite pet

1 Wie kannst du dein Lieblingshaustier beschreiben?
Kreise die passenden Wörter in den Wolken ein.

Colour: It is ...

brown, orange, grey, black, white, blue

Body parts: It has got ...

a head, a tail, four legs, no legs, wings, long ears

Food: It likes ...

water, grains, carrots, bones, cat food, dog food, mice, fish flakes

2 Beschreibe dein Lieblingshaustier. Ergänze die Satzanfänge mit deinen eingekreisten Wörtern.

All about my favourite pet

My favourite pet is a ______

It is ______

It has got ______

It likes ______

______

3 Präsentiere dein Lieblingshaustier.

This is my favourite pet.

Honey page – Pets

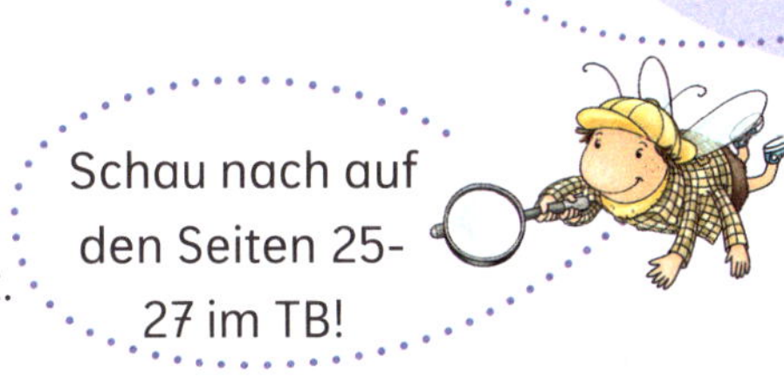

1 Das sind meine wichtigsten Wörter zum Thema Haustiere.
Schreibe die Wörter in den Rahmen, die du dir merken möchtest.

2 Ich kann meine Lieblingshaustiere aufzählen.

I like ____.

My favourite pet is a ______________________________________.

3 Ich kann mich über Haustiere unterhalten.

At the shopping centre

pineapple, pencil, hamster, toaster, bacon and eggs, trousers, cap

1 Welcher Gegenstand ist jeweils falsch im Bild? Umkreise ihn.

2 Schreibe die Wörter jeweils auf die Linien.

pineapple

b

h

t

3 Umkreise das Wort, das nicht in die Reihe passt.

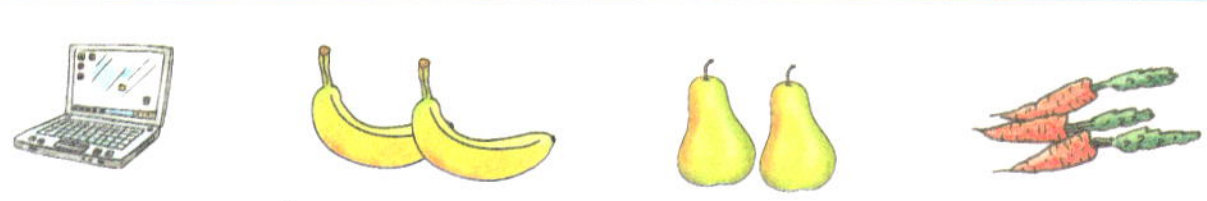

1. laptop - bananas - pears - carrots

2. rabbit - mouse - dress - cat

4 Hier findest du drei Wörter zum Thema Kleidung. Füge ein Wort hinzu, das nicht zum Thema passt.

skirt - trousers - ______________________ - raincoat

Shopping

1 Lies die Wörter.

2 Kreise alle Lebensmittel grün und alle Kleidungsstücke rot ein. Schreibe die Wörter auf.

bananas	dress	carrots	pineapples	trousers	shoes
cheese	butter	T-shirt	cornflakes	raincoat	skirt

butter, pineapples

b ______, c ______

c ______, c ______

dress, raincoat

t ______, s ______

T ______, s ______

3 Beschrifte die Gegenstände.

t ______ C ______ h ______

charger

c ______ p ______ l ______

CD	computer	laptop	tablet	~~charger~~	phone	headphones

LET'S PRACTISE! Shopping dialogue

1. Höre dir den Dialog mehrmals an.
2. Höre dir den Dialog nochmals an und lies die Sprechblasen mit. Nummeriere die Sprechblasen in der richtigen Reihenfolge (1-9).
3. Übe den Dialog.
4. Spiele den Dialog mit einem Partnerkind nach.

1 Hello!

Hm, I don't like them. What about the red T-shirt? How much is it?

Bye!

I'd like to buy a pair of shoes.

Thank you. Goodbye!

It's 2 pounds.

2 Hello! Can I help you?

Okay! Here you are.

Look here are some nice sports shoes.

CD 57

No T-shirt for Cameron?

1 Höre dir die Geschichte nochmals an.

2 Lies die Sätze und kreuze die richtigen Wörter an.

3 Vergleiche mit einem Partnerkind.

Schau nach auf Seite 35 in deinem TB.

1. Cameron talks to	◯ Emma.	◯ Marcus.
2. They go to	◯ the supermarket.	◯ the new sports shop.
3. Cameron's size is	◯ small.	◯ pink.
4. Cameron thinks orange is	◯ great.	◯ awful.
5. His friend wants to go	◯ to the snack bar.	◯ to school.
6. Cameron's favourite colour is	◯ a pencil case.	◯ blue.
7. On his T-shirt there is	◯ a spaceship.	◯ a dinosaur.
8. The new T-shirt is	◯ 5 pounds.	◯ 8 pounds.

4 Höre dir das Ende der Geschichte an. Kreuze das richtige Bild an.

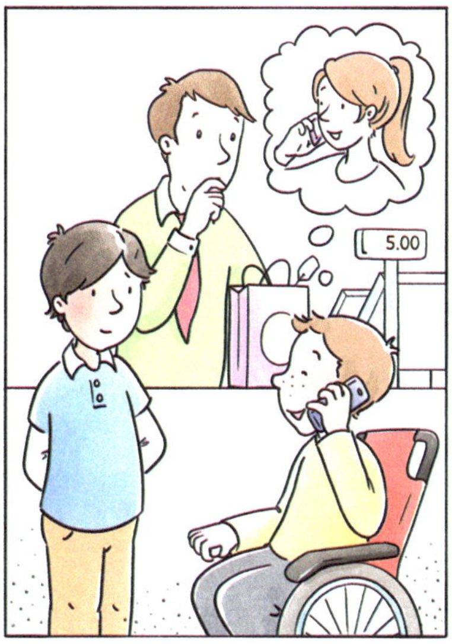

◯

◯

CD 59-60

Breakfast with Ben's family

1 Höre dir das Lied an.

2 Markiere die Schlüsselwörter und verbinde sie mit dem Bild.

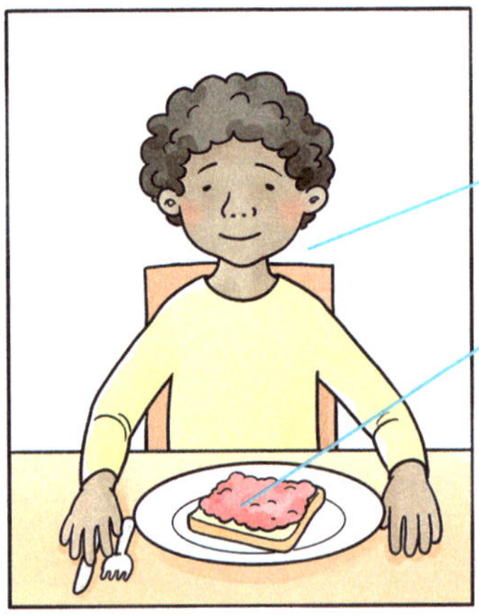

Ben is at the table.

Jam is on his plate.

Now it's time for breakfast.

He isn't late.

Mum is at the table.

Cheese is on her plate.

Now it's time for breakfast.

She isn't late.

Dad is at the table.

Bacon is on his plate.

Now it's time for breakfast.

He isn't late.

isn't = is not

Honey page – At the shopping centre

1 Das sind meine wichtigsten Wörter zum Thema Einkaufen.
Schreibe die Wörter in den Rahmen, die du dir merken möchtest.

Schau nach auf den Seiten 33 und 34 im TB!

2 Ich kann über mein Lieblingseis berichten und es bestellen.

What's your favourite ice cream? - My favourite ice cream is

____.

What can I do for you? - I'd like two scoops of______________________________

____ in a cone, please.

3 Ich kann fragen wieviel etwas kostet.

How much is/are ... ?

That's ... pounds.

A trip to London

1 Spielt das Spiel.

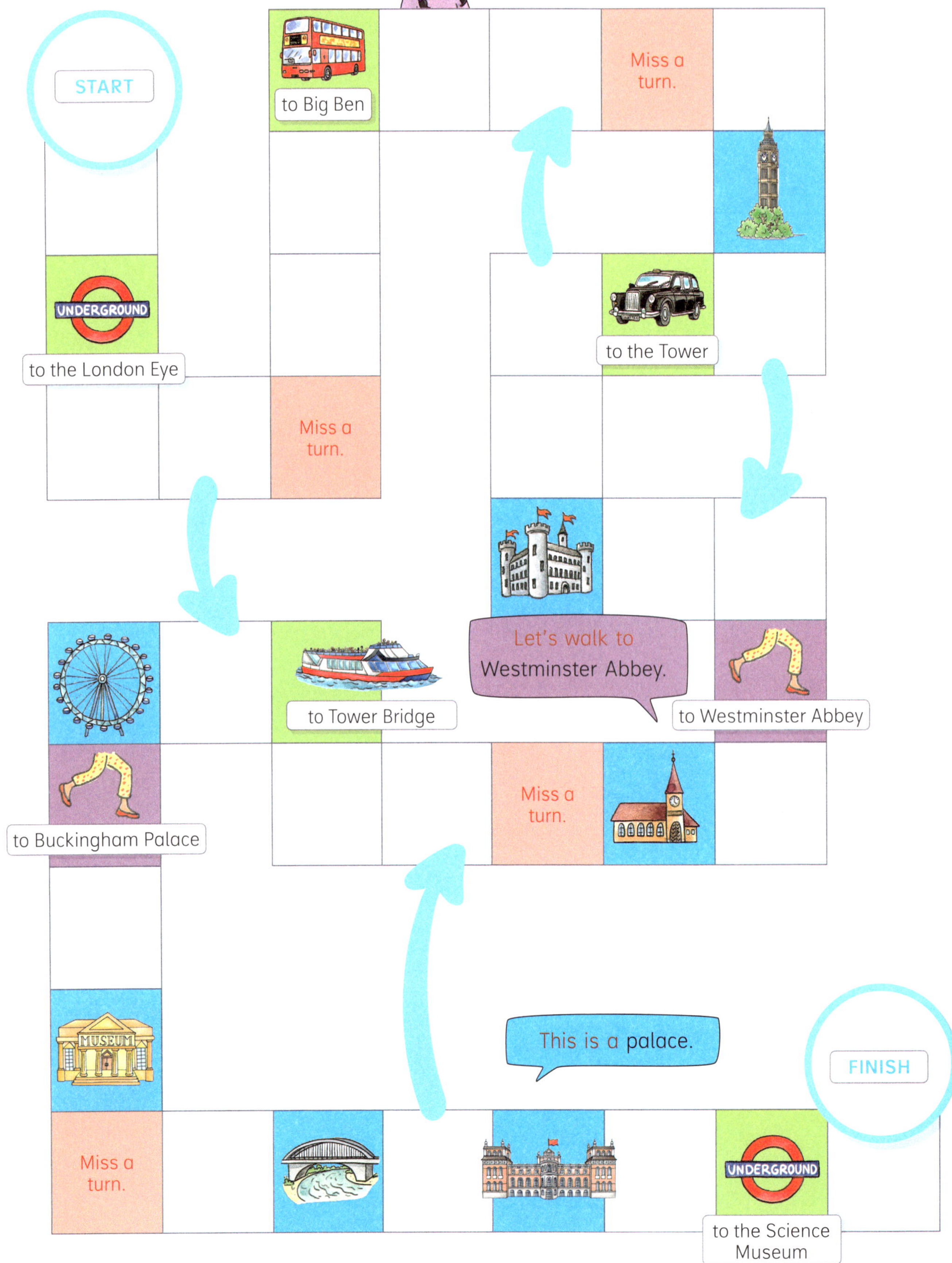

A visit from Scotland

Schau nach auf Seite 38 im TB.

1 Lies und kreuze die richtigen Wörter an.

1. Emma's cousin is coming to London.
His name is ...
- ◯ Anna. L
- ◯ David. R

2. Her cousin and his family are coming for ...
- ◯ three days. E
- ◯ a week. O

3. They are coming ...
- ◯ by taxi. F
- ◯ by train. C

4. On a sunny day Mrs Brown would like to go to ...
- ◯ Hyde Park. K
- ◯ London Zoo. W

5. Mike would like to visit the ...
- ◯ Science Museum. E
- ◯ London Eye. Z

6. Emma would like to go ...
- ◯ on a bus trip. P
- ◯ on a boat trip. T

2 Trage die Lösungsbuchstaben von Aufgabe 1 ein. Schreibe das Lösungswort.

1	2	3	4	5	6
R					

Mike wants to show David the R_ _ _ _ _ _ in the Science Museum.

LET'S PRACTISE!

What would you like to do in Hyde Park?

1 Höre die CD an und nummeriere die Wörter.

☐ have a picnic

☐ play croquet

☐ take photos

☐ play football

1 walk the dog

☐ buy an ice cream

2 Höre dir den Dialog an und übe ihn.

What would you like to do in Hyde Park?

I'd like to have a picnic.

I'd like to take photos. How about you?

3 Befrage 2 Kinder.

name						
______						
______						

The London Eye

1 Höre die CD an und lies den Text mit.

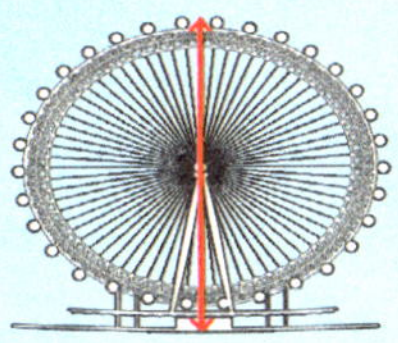

The London Eye is the **biggest ferris wheel** in Europe.

It was built **in 1999**.

It is **135 metres high**.

LONDON EYE

It is **120 metres in diameter**.

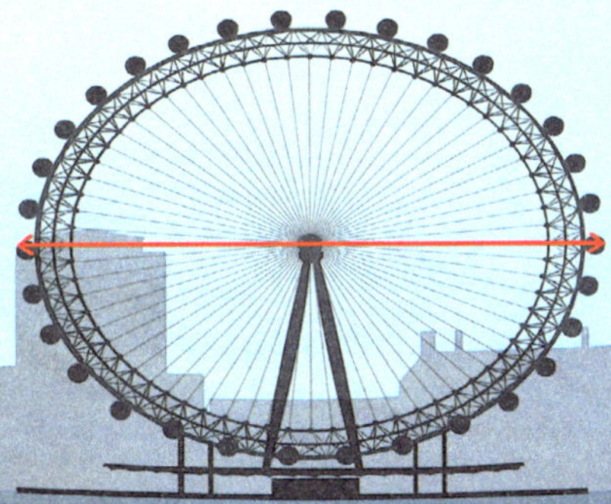

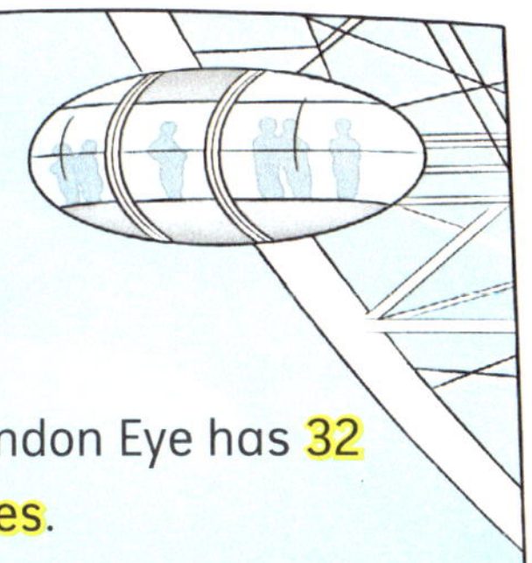

The London Eye has **32 capsules**.

25 people fit in one capsule.

One round in the London Eye takes **30 minutes**.

2 Beantworte die Fragen.

Was ist das London Eye?	
Wann wurde es gebaut?	
Wie hoch ist das London Eye?	135 m
Wie groß ist der Durchmesser?	
Wie viele Gondeln hat das London Eye?	
Wie viele Personen passen in eine Gondel?	
Wie lange dauert eine Umdrehung im London Eye?	

3 Vergleiche mit einem Partnerkind.

CD 75

A postcard

1 Lies die Postkarte.

Dear Ian,
London is great!
The weather is sunny.
My cousin Emma and I are on a sightseeing tour today.
I like Tower Bridge, Big Ben and the London Eye best.
It's really cool!

See you, David

Ian Stafford
5, Palmerston Road
Dublin 14
Republic of Ireland

2 Lies die Postkarte nochmals und kreuze Davids Lieblingssehenswürdigkeiten an.

 ◯

 ◯

 ◯

 ◯

 ◯

 ◯

3 Schreibe deine eigene Postkarte.

Dear ______________________,

London is ______________________!

The weather is ______________________.

My ______________________

and I are on a sightseeing tour today.

I like ______________________

____

______________________ best.

See you, ______________________

____

____

____

____

London is...
great • exciting • interesting • cool ...

The weather is...
rainy • foggy • windy ...

My ...
cousin • friend • brother • sister ...

I like...
the Tower of London • Big Ben • Buckingham Palace • ...

Honey page – A trip to London

1 Das sind meine wichtigsten Wörter zum Thema London.
Schreibe die Wörter in den Rahmen, die du dir merken möchtest.

Schau nach auf den Seiten 39-42 im TB!

 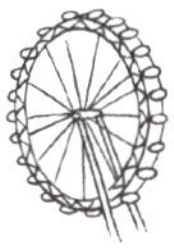  

2 Ich kann die Sehenswürdigkeiten erklären. Verbinde die Satzteile richtig.

The Tower of London	is the palace of the royal family.
Buckingham Palace	is a bridge over the River Thames.
Tower Bridge	is a big ferris wheel.
The London Eye	is a museum showing the Crown Jewels.

3 Ich kann mich darüber unterhalten, was man in London machen kann.

What would you like to do in London?

I'd like to see Big Ben.

I'd like to see ____________________

____

LET'S PRACTISE!

What's the weather like?

1 Höre die CD an und lies den Dialog mit.

2 Male das passende Wettersymbol in die Kästchen. Vergleiche mit einem Partnerkind.

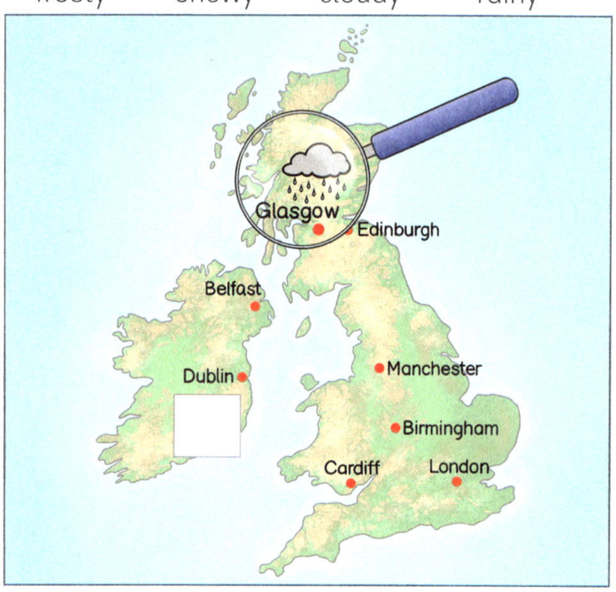

spring

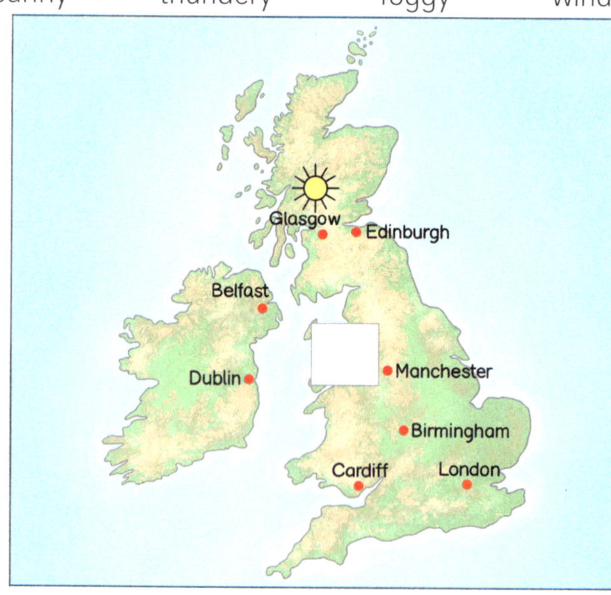

summer

autumn

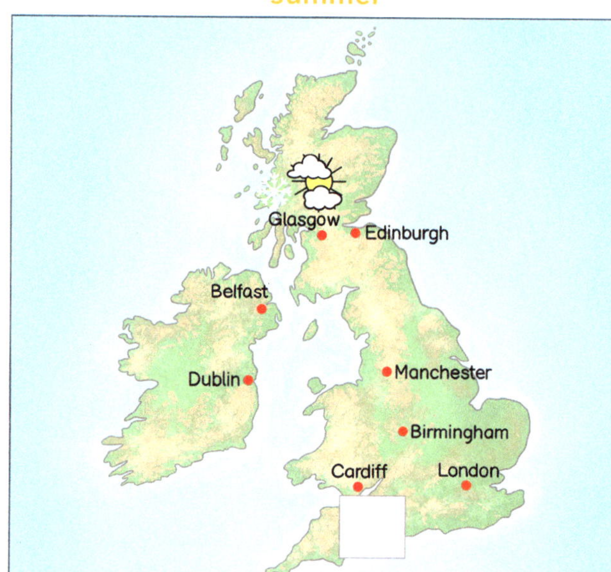

winter

CD 81

Emma's birthday party

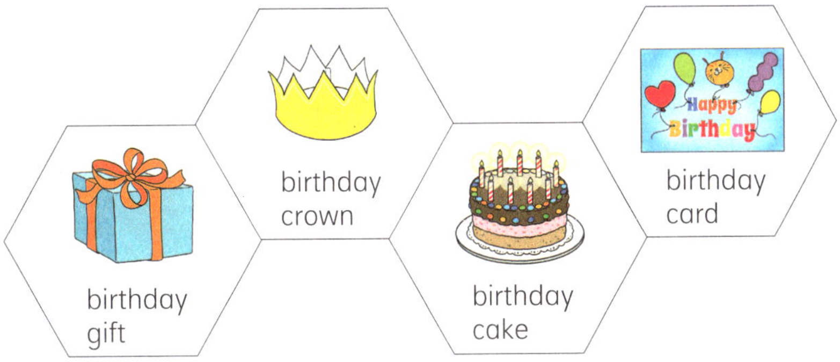

Pupil's Audio-CD 35

1 Höre die CD an und zeige auf die beschriebenen Gegenstände.

2 Lies die Sätze und kreuze an, ob sie wahr oder falsch sind.

There are 6 muffins on the table.		
There is a pink birthday cake.		
Emma's friends eat cucumbers.		
There are 3 gifts on the table.		
Lisa and Ben have a nice birthday card for Emma.		

CD 82
KV 78
Fö 32

Halloween: A ghost story

1. Höre dir die Geschichte an und zeige auf die Bilder.
2. Worum geht es in der Geschichte? Erzähle auf Deutsch.
3. Vervollständige das letzte Bild.

Decorate a Christmas tree

1 Spielt das Spiel und vervollständigt den Weihnachtsbaum.

2 Beschreibe deinen Weihnachtsbaum.

On my Christmas tree I've got ...

How to make pancakes

1 Höre die CD an und zeige auf das richtige Bild.

2 Höre die CD nochmals an und nummeriere die Bilder.

Easter partner dictation

1 Male 4 farbige Ostereier in Bild A.

2 Sage deinem Partnerkind, wo deine Ostereier sind. Dein Partnerkind soll sie in Bild B malen. Dann ist dein Partnerkind an der Reihe.

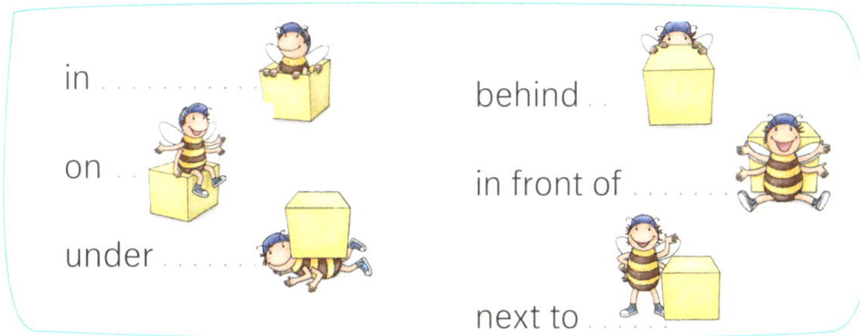

A

B

Numbers 1

1 Höre die CD an und sprich die Zahlen nach.

Pupil's Audio-CD 41

11 eleven

12 twelve

13 thirteen

14 fourteen

15 fifteen

16 sixteen

17 seventeen

18 eighteen

19 nineteen

2 Höre die CD an. Verbinde den Sperrmüll mit den Häusern.

Numbers 2

1 Höre die CD an und sprich die Zahlen nach.

Pupil's Audio-CD 42

20	twenty
30	thirty
40	forty
50	fifty
60	sixty
70	seventy
80	eighty
90	ninety
100	one hundred

2 Schreibe das Ergebnis auf.

20	+	1	=	21
twenty		one		twenty-one
30	+	8	=	38
thirty		eight		thirty-eight
40	+	2	=	42
forty		two		
60	+	5	=	65
sixty		five		
80	+	6	=	86
eighty		six		

3 Höre die CD an und schreibe die Zahlen auf.

14 ______ ______ ______ ______ ______ ______ ______

Fit for 4!

1 Schaue dir das Bild 1 auf Seite 54 in deinem Textbook an. Lies die Fragen und trage das gesuchte Wort ein. Die Wörterbox hilft dir.

Across →
1 What are the boys playing?
2 What season is it?
3 What animals are swimming in the pond?
4 Where are all the people?
5 What are the man and the woman doing?

Down ↓
1 What are the children taking for a walk?
2 Where are the goldfish?
3 What can you buy at the candy van?
4 What are the football players wearing?
5 How many boys are playing football?

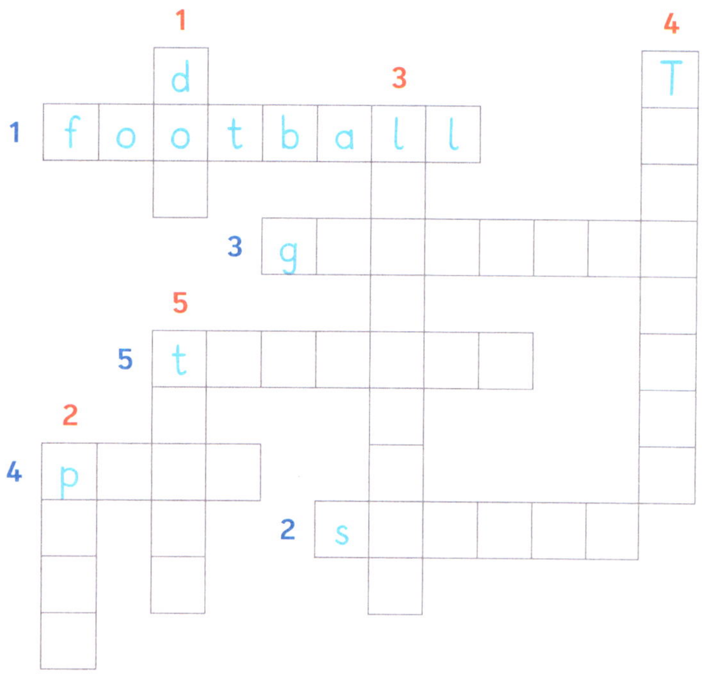

~~football~~	dog
park	lollipops
goldfish	T-shirts
talking	pond
spring	three

2 Lies die Sätze und nummeriere das Bild.

1 A place where you can buy ice cream.

2 Two people are playing with boats.

3 A person is on inline skates.

4 Two people are lying in the sun.

5 Five baby ducks are swimming in the pond.

6 Was stimmt nicht im Bild?

Fit for 4!

1 Schaue dir das Bild 3 auf Seite 55 in deinem Textbook an. Lies die Fragen und verbinde sie mit den richtigen Antworten.

1	What season is it?	**d**	At the stall.
2	Who is flying the wonderful kites?	**y**	The Easter nest.
3	What colour are the horses?	**a**	There are three ducks.
4	Where can you buy sandwiches?	**w**	It's autumn.
5	Who is just buying a cheese sandwich?	**n**	They are brown.
6	What is the family feeding?	**i**	Two children.
7	How many ducks are there in the pond?	**y**	An old lady.
8	Was stimmt nicht im Bild?	**d**	The ducks in the pond.

2 Write the solution.

It's a

1	2	3	4	5
w				

6	7	8

3 Schaue dir das Bild 4 auf Seite 55 in deinem Textbook an. Lies die Sätze und kreise die richtigen Wörter ein.

1. It is a cold day in summer / winter.
2. You can buy cold / warm drinks at the stall.
3. Two boys and a girl are / One boy is playing ice hockey on the pond.
4. One child is making an Easter man / a snowman.
5. Three children are having a snowball / a strawberry fight.
6. A man and a little girl / a lady are coming back from a shopping tour.

4 Schreibe drei Sätze mit den richtigen Wörtern ab.

The correct sentences

Classroom phrases

My words

colours

- red
- orange
- yellow
- green
- blue
- purple
- pink
- brown
- white
- black
- grey

numbers

- zero 0
- one 1
- two 2
- three 3
- four 4
- five 5
- six 6
- seven 7
- eight 8
- nine 9
- ten 10
- eleven 11
- twelve 12

feelings

- fine
- happy
- sad
- tired

Die Zahlen 13–100 findest du auf den Seiten 46 und 47 im WB!

school things

- school bag
- rubber
- ruler
- pencil
- scissors
- coloured pencils
- pencil case
- pen
- glue stick
- sharpener
- book
- folder
- lunch box
- chair
- table

rooms and furniture

hall . . . .

living room . . . .

kitchen . . . .

bedroom . . . .

bathroom . . . .

sofa . . . .

bed . . . .

lamp . . . .

bookshelf . . . .

wardrobe . . . .

washbasin . . . .

toilet . . . .

shower . . . .

fridge . . . .

cooker . . . .

family

brother . . . .

sister . . . .

father . . . .

mother . . . .

grandfather . . . .

grandmother . . . .

prepositions

in . . . .

on . . . .

under . . . .

behind . . . .

in front of . . . .

next to . . . .

feelings

proud . . . .

angry . . . .

excited . . . .

days of the week

Monday . . . . MON

Tuesday . . . . TUE

Wednesday . . . . WED

Thursday . . . . THU

Friday . . . . FRI

Saturday . . . . SAT

Sunday . . . . SUN

Diff ▲ L kann zusätzlich zum Einsatz von Bildwörterbüchern oder Online-Wörterbüchern anregen.

hobbies

playing football ...... 

playing table tennis .... 

drawing .... 

swimming ... 

horse riding .... 

skateboarding .... 

biking .... 

dancing .... 

playing computer games .... 

reading .... 

playing an instrument ...... 

collecting stickers ... 

playing hockey .... 

playing cards .... 

meeting friends .... 

pets and body parts

dog ...... 

cat .... 

mouse .... 

mice .... 

hamster .... 

rabbit .... 

goldfish .... 

guinea pig ...... 

budgie ..... 

rat .... 

mouth ...... 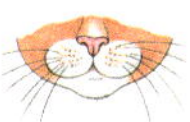

nose .... 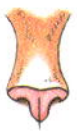

eyes .... 

ears .... 

legs .... 

tail .... 

pet food

cucumbers ..... 

water .... 

rice .... 

pet food .... 

grains .... 

bones .... 

carrots .... 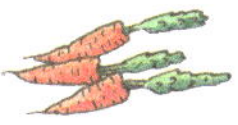

clothes

skirt 

trousers 

dress 

raincoat 

shoes 

put on 

take off 

food

cheese 

jam 

bread 

butter 

cereals 

bacon and eggs 

apple 

pear 

pineapple 

vanilla ice cream 

chocolate ice cream 

strawberry ice cream 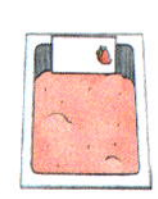

hazelnut ice cream 

cherry ice cream 

lemon ice cream 

kiwi ice cream 

blue angel ice cream 

media

CD 

computer 

laptop 

tablet 

phone 

charger 

headphones 

English money

pounds 

pence 

sights, transport and activities

- palace
- church
- bridge
- ferris wheel
- castle
- museum
- underground
- taxi
- double-decker bus
- train
- boat
- walk
- take a photo
- visit
- see

seasons and weather

- spring
- summer
- autumn
- winter
- frosty
- snowy
- cloudy
- rainy
- warm
- sunny
- hot
- thundery
- cold
- foggy
- windy

Special days

birthday

- birthday gift
- birthday crown
- birthday cake
- birthday card

Halloween

- ghost
- pumpkin
- bat
- skeleton
- spider
- vampire
- witch

Christmas

- Christmas tree
- Father Christmas
- angel
- star
- bell
- candle
- reindeer
- bauble
- Christmas stocking

Easter

- Easter egg
- Easter basket
- Easter bunny
- bush
- tree
- bench

Bumblebee

Workbook Förderausgabe für Englisch in Klasse 3

Bildquellennachweis:
|Alamy Stock Photo (RMB), Abingdon/Oxfordshire: Ball, David 38.3; Hornak, Angelo 38.2; Kuttig 38.1; moyano, juan 3.16; Segre, Alex 35.5; Turner, Bob 38.5. |Colourbox.com, Odense: Monkey Business Images 35.1. |fotolia.com, New York: 300dpi 3.6; Kramin, V. 3.15; Licht und Blindheit 38.4; NilsZ 3.12; OHRAUGE 38.6; samuelkruszewski 36.2; sveta 3.11; zhu difeng 29.2; zjk 29.1. |iStockphoto.com, Calgary: Ferrao, José Manuel 3.14; gmnicholas 3.4; Grassetto 3.1; JohanJK 19.3; ma-k 3.7; simonbradfield 35.2; studiocasper 3.3. |Shutterstock.com, New York: Amat, Aaron 3.8; Barton, Willy 35.4; ESLINE 19.1; Heim, Ramona 19.5; Stockforlife 3.5; stockphoto-graf 3.13. |stock.adobe.com, Dublin: Ben-Ari, Rafael 35.3; emuck 3.10; Fischer, Magda 3.2; Kostic, Dusan 19.2; sergojpg 3.9. |Tauber, Andreas, Berlin: 5.1, 5.2, 5.3, 5.4, 5.5, 5.6, 5.7, 5.8, 5.9, 5.10, 5.11, 6.1, 6.2, 7.1, 7.2, 9.1, 9.2, 9.3, 11.1, 15.1, 15.2, 15.3, 18.1, 18.2, 18.3, 21.1, 21.2, 23.1, 26.1, 27.1, 27.2, 30.1, 30.2, 36.1, 37.1, 39.1, 39.2, 40.1, 40.2, 45.1. |vario images, Bonn: Uppercut 19.4.

Texte soweit nicht anders angegeben: Gisela Ehlers, Grit Kahstein, Christina Meindl, Ursula Michailow-Drews, Anna Van Montagu, Matthias Muth, Michaela Schönau, Hannelore Tait, Anne Zeich-Pelsis

Musiknachweis Pupil's Audio-CD:
1/2: Bumblebee rap ℗ © Westermann Bildungsmedien Verlag. **3/4:** The colour song ℗ © Westermann Bildungsmedien Verlag. **9/10:** Together. Text/Musik: Mark und Helen Johnson © Out of the Ark Ltd. Arrangement: Karl-F. Parnow-Kloth, tonpumpe, Lüneburg ℗ Westermann Bildungsmedien Verlag. **14/15:** Harry the hamster. Text: Wolle Kriwanek / Musik und Arrangement: Wolle Kriwanek, Jörg Orlamünder, Michael Schwarz ℗ © Westermann Bildungsmedien Verlag. **17/18:** Reach for the sky. Text/Musik: Pamela Conn Beall, Susan Hagen Nipp from WEE SING CHILDREN'S SONGS AND FINGERPLAYS by Pamela Conn Beall and Susan Hagen Nipp, illustrated by Nancy Spence Klein, copyright © 1977, 1979 by Pamela Conn Beall and Susan Hagen Nipp. Used by permission of Price Stern Sloan, an imprint of Penguin Publishing Group, a division of Penguin Random House LLC. All rights reserved. ℗ Westermann Bildungsmedien Verlag. **21/22:** Weekend is here. Text: Wolle Kriwanek / Musik und Arrangement: Wolle Kriwanek, Jörg Orlamünder, Michael Schwarz ℗ © Westermann Bildungsmedien Verlag. **25/26:** Animal rap ℗ © Westermann Bildungsmedien Verlag. **29/30:** Breakfast chant ℗ © Westermann Bildungsmedien Verlag. **38/39:** I hear them. Text/Musik: traditionell. ℗ © Westermann Bildungsmedien Verlag.

Druck A^4 / Jahr 2024
Alle Drucke der Serie A sind im Unterricht parallel verwendbar.

Redaktion: Tisa Purackal, Lena Schmidt
Umschlaggestaltung: Visuelle Lebensfreude, Hannover, mit Illustrationen von Friederike Schumann
Layout: Visuelle Lebensfreude, Hannover
Druck und Bindung: Westermann Druck GmbH, Georg-Westermann-Allee 66, 38104 Braunschweig

ISBN 978-3-14-**126902**-4